READING

SEAHORSE CONNECTIONS

HELPING MY CHILD

A Guide to Supporting School Readiness Skills

GRADE PRE-K

SEAHORSE PUBLISHING

TABLE OF CONTENTS

THE SCIENCE OF READING

Reading is an essential skill for success in school and in life. In order to understand how children learn to read, parents should understand the science of reading.

The *science of reading* is a term that refers to more than 20 years of research by experts on how people learn to read. The research shows that reading does not come naturally. For many people, it takes significant effort. Learning how to read is most effective when it happens in a step-by-step process that is based on proven, research-supported strategies and techniques.

Good reading instruction is more than just learning to sound out words. It helps students develop skills in phonological awareness, phonics, fluency, vocabulary, and comprehension. All these skills help students build pathways in their brains that connect speech sounds to print and that connect words with their meanings. By using the science of reading as a guide, parents and teachers can support our children in learning how to read.

KEYS TO EFFECTIVE READING INSTRUCTION

Phonological Awareness: The ability to notice, think about, and work with the sounds that make up spoken words

Phonics: Understanding the relationship between sounds and the letters that represent them in written words

Fluency: The ability to read quickly and accurately

Vocabulary: Understanding word meanings

Comprehension: Gaining meaning from reading

SHOULD MY CHILD BE ABLE TO READ BEFORE KINDERGARTEN?

Each child develops at their own pace. They should not be pushed to read before they are developmentally ready. Children may become frustrated if they are pressured to read too soon. This can result in a child not wanting to read at all. Your child will show you they are ready by responding well to encouragement and by quickly learning skills.

SCARBOROUGH'S READING ROPE

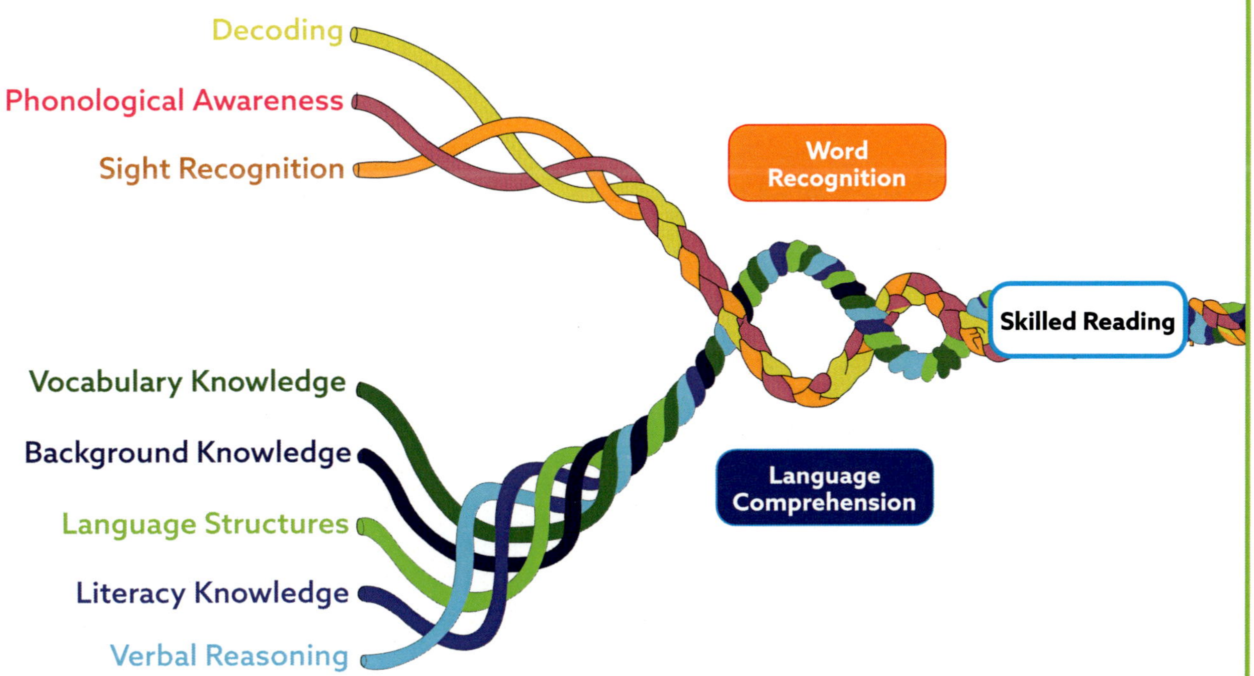

To show how children draw on a variety of abilities to become skilled readers, Dr. Hollis Scarborough created the Reading Rope. In 2001, this model was published in the *Handbook of Early Literacy Research* (Neuman/Dickinson).

ORAL LANGUAGE: THE FOUNDATION OF LITERACY

People are born to speak. Almost all children learn the rules of their native language at an early age without formal instruction. They work through the rules of language on their own. A child who says, "I goed there before" will quickly learn to say, "I went there before." As their oral language skills develop, children are also using words to make sense of their experiences and to form connections with others.

Although your child is not yet reading, they are laying the groundwork for literacy by listening, talking to others, and engaging in pretend play. The environment plays an important factor in how children learn. You can help your child build early comprehension skills by having meaningful conversations, reading books aloud, and taking time to discuss what you read.

ORAL LANGUAGE CHECKLIST

Your prekindergartner is well on their way to mastering these oral language skills. If you are concerned about your child's development in any of these areas, please contact a speech language pathologist or other experts.

- ✔ Speaks in sentences of about four words and also uses some longer sentences.
- ✔ Uses plural nouns correctly (examples: ducks, dishes).
- ✔ Uses pronouns correctly (examples: they, he, hers).
- ✔ Follows basic, two-step directions.
- ✔ Answers *what*, *who*, and *where* questions.
- ✔ Asks *why*, *when*, and *how* questions.

ACTIVITIES FOR BUILDING ORAL LANGUAGE SKILLS

TO CORRECT OR NOT TO CORRECT?

Instead of correcting your child's speech, model standard language as you expand on your child's comment. If your child says, "Me eat kawots," you can provide a model with the response, "Yes. I eat carrots. You eat carrots. They are crunchy."

WALK AND TALK

Walk through your neighborhood and encourage your child to point out things to talk about. Ask open-ended questions that begin with *who, what, why, where, when*, and *how*.

TELL ME MORE

Prompt your child with questions that require more than a "yes" or "no" answer. If your child says, "I saw a dog," you can reply, "Tell me more. Where do you think the dog was going? Why?"

ACT IT OUT

After reading a story to your child, act it out together. Use stuffed animals, action figures, and other props you find around the house.

ACTIVE TALKING

Make the most of everyday conversations by modeling language for your child. You might say, "Let's put on our shoes so we can go to the park." Follow up with an open-ended question for your child such as, "Since we are going to the park, what would you like to bring?"

I CAN TELL YOU ABOUT...

Choose something to learn more about with your child, such as dogs, the ocean, or helpers in the community. Take out books from the library to read together or use internet sources. Try to learn five new facts. Have your child share the facts with the rest of the family.

PHONOLOGICAL AND PHONEMIC AWARENESS: HEARING SOUNDS IN WORDS

Phonological awareness and phonemic awareness are important pre-reading skills. They describe a child's ability to hear, identify, and play with sounds in spoken language. These skills form an essential foundation for reading and writing development in kindergarten and beyond.

Children demonstrate phonological awareness when they recognize and manipulate, or change, parts of spoken words. Phonemic awareness is the last phonological awareness skill to develop. Children who have mastered phonemic awareness can hear, recognize, and play with the individual sounds, or phonemes, in spoken words.

PHONOLOGICAL AWARENESS MILESTONES

Ages 3 to 4	Produces real and pretend rhyming words
Ages 4 to 5	Claps or taps out syllables in words Recognizes words that begin with the same sound Segments or separates out each sound in words with three sounds Blends or combines individual sounds to produce words that have three sounds Counts the number of sounds in words that have three sounds
Ages 5 to 6	Segments or separates out each sound in words with four sounds Identifies the first and last sounds in a word Groups words with the same beginning sound Identifies which word does not rhyme in a set of three words Identifies which word is not the same in a set of three words
Ages 6 to 7	Deletes syllables from words when asked Deletes sounds from words when asked Substitutes syllables in words when asked Substitutes sounds in words when asked
Ages 7 to 8	Uses phonological awareness skills to spell words

ACTIVITIES FOR BUILDING PHONOLOGICAL AWARENESS

SYLLABLE HUNT

Look around the house to find things whose names have more than one syllable. Say the word and hold up a finger for each word part. For example, say, "bed-room" for bedroom and "ma-ca-ro-ni" for macaroni.

SWITCH IT

Think of a one-syllable word. Ask your child to change the beginning, middle, or ending sound in the word to make a new word. Use this example, reading letters shown in between slash marks as sounds.

Parent: Change the /m/ sound in *mop* to /h/. What is the new word?

Child: Hop.

Parent: Great job! Now, change the /ŭ/ sound in *hut* to /ă/. What is the new word?

Child: Hat.

Parent: Excellent thinking. Try changing the /d/ sound in *bed* to /g/. What is the new word?

Child: Beg.

Parent: Terrific! You did it!

RHYME TIME

Rhyming is an important phonemic awareness skill. Use these ideas to help your child practice rhyming.

Rhyme Train: Say two words that rhyme. Ask your child to say a third rhyming word. Accept your child's addition even if it is not a real word. Keep going with more rhyming pairs.

Raise for a Rhyme: Say rhyming and non-rhyming word pairs. Ask your child to raise their hand only when they hear words that rhyme.

Find the Pair: Say three words: two that rhyme and one that doesn't. Have your child tell you which two words rhyme.

PHONICS: LETTERS MAKE SOUNDS

Phonics is the knowledge that letters and combinations of letters represent sounds. This is an essential skill for beginning readers.

All words are made up of sounds. The word *dog* has three sounds. Each letter stands for one sound. The word *light* has three sounds. The letters *igh* represent one sound. The English language uses 44 sounds to make all words. However, there are only 26 letters in the alphabet. Some letters can make more than one sound. Other letters combine to make new sounds. This is like a code that beginning readers must figure out.

Prekindergartners are just beginning to understand the phonics code. They learn the letters of the alphabet and start to associate a sound with each one. By the time they are ready to start kindergarten, they should know most of the consonant sounds and short vowel sounds.

PHONICS 101

CONSONANT OR VOWEL?

Consonant letters are *b, c, d, f, g, h, j, k, l, m, n, p, q, r, s, t, v, w, x, y* (as in *you*), and *z*.

Vowel letters are *a, e, i, o, u,* and *y* (as in *my* and *baby*). Short vowels are marked with a curved symbol, like a smile on top: /ă/. Long vowels are marked with a horizontal line on top: /ā/.

ACTIVITIES FOR BUILDING PHONICS SKILLS

SHAVING CREAM LETTERS

Squirt shaving cream onto a large baking sheet. Spread it around evenly. Choose a letter and make its sound. Use a finger to write the letter in the shaving cream and say its name. Say the sound the letter makes as you underline it. You can also do this with whipped cream!

SHORT VOWELS IN ACTION

Help your child remember short vowel sounds by associating an action with each one.

A: Pretend to bite an apple. Say, "I see a worm in my apple! Aaaah! Short *a* says /ă/ like what we said when we saw a worm in our apple!"

E: Slide your finger back and forth along the edge of a table. Say, "Eh-eh-edge. Short *e* says /ĕ/ like the beginning sound in *edge*."

I: Scratch your nose. Say, "I have an ih-ih-itch. Short *i* says /ĭ/ like the beginning sound in *itch*."

O: Open your mouth as if the doctor is checking your throat. Say, "Ahhhh. Short *o* says /ŏ/ like the sound you make at the doctor."

U: Point upward. Say, "Uh-uh-up. Short *u* says /ŭ/ like the beginning sound in *up*."

KEEP IT SHORT

To avoid confusing beginning readers, don't add a vowel sound when you make consonant sounds. For example, the sound for letter *t* is /t/, not /tuh/.

RAINBOW LETTERS

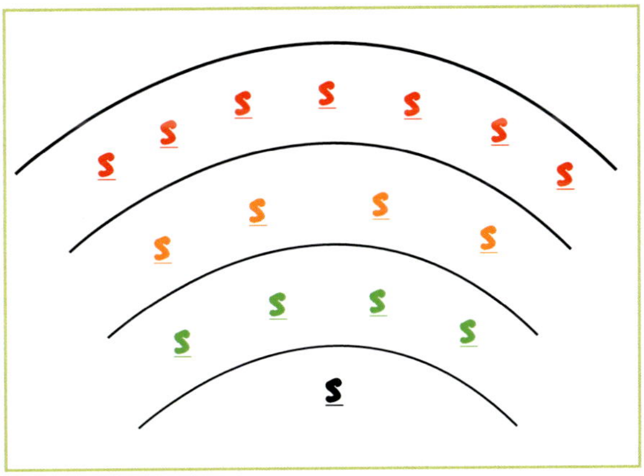

Draw a set of rainbow arches with space in between. Write a letter under the rainbow. Then, begin with the top arch. Use a red marker or crayon.

Follow these steps:

1. Say the sound the letter makes.
2. Write the letter and say its name as you write.
3. Underline the letter and say the sound it makes.

Repeat until the first arch is filled. Then, use an orange marker or crayon to fill the second arch in the same way as you say, write and spell, underline and read. Repeat for the next arches using different colors.

MAKE A MATCH

Make one set of cards with alphabet letters and another set with pictures whose names begin with the letters. Mix up all the cards and place them facedown. Take turns flipping over pairs. When someone makes a match, remember to say the letter name, the letter sound, and the picture name. Example: b, /b/, ball.

VOCABULARY: WORDS HAVE MEANING

Vocabulary plays a critical role in the process of learning to read. Young readers use their knowledge about words to make sense of what they are reading. In order to understand what is read, a child must know what the words mean. Children need a large mental "word bank" to draw on as they read. The larger a child's vocabulary, the more they are able to comprehend what they are reading or listening to.

As new words are encountered, children link them to words they already know to add to their growing vocabularies. Some words are learned naturally. Others must be taught. Children learn new words through daily conversations and by having experiences that teach them about the world. Reading books to your child also exposes them to rich language.

MY VOCABULARY JOURNAL

Have your child keep a vocabulary journal. Use a spiral-bound notebook or composition book. Write one vocabulary word on each page. Draw or find a picture that represents the word.

TYPES OF VOCABULARY

Listening Vocabulary: The words we hear
Speaking Vocabulary: The words we say
Reading Vocabulary: The words we read
Writing Vocabulary: The words we use to write

ACTIVITIES FOR BUILDING VOCABULARY

NEW WORD TALK

Introduce a new word to your child by providing a simple definition. Then, give an example that relates to your child's experiences. Have your child think of an example, too. Over the next few days, take the opportunity to use the new word in conversation.

WORDS FROM NONFICTION

Choose a nonfiction book. Read the book aloud to your child. Talk about new words from the book. Have your child share with others the new words they learned.

NEW WORDS WHILE READING

When your child is listening to a story, it is okay to stop to discuss a new word. Reread the sentence and ask what your child thinks the new word means. Give a child-friendly definition. Help your child make a personal connection to the word.

COMPREHENSION: UNDERSTANDING WHAT IS READ ALOUD

Reading comprehension is the essence of reading. It is the ability to gain meaning from what you read. This is a complex skill that develops over time. As you read to your child, encourage them to think about what they are hearing. For good comprehension, their mind must be "turned on" and thinking actively.

Prekindergartners are absorbing lots of information as they listen to books and learn about the world around them. They can show their understanding of fiction books by retelling a story and describing its characters, setting, and events. They can show their understanding of nonfiction books by telling important facts they learned about a topic.

ACTIVE READING

Active reading happens when the reader is involved and engaged with the text. The reader is thinking about what is being read and making connections. This type of reading is essential for comprehension.

You can help your child become an active reader by remembering A-B-C.

A: Ask questions about the reading.

B: Build vocabulary by learning new words from the reading.

C: Connect the reading to your child's own experiences.

ACTIVITIES FOR BUILDING READING COMPREHENSION

MAKE A NOTE (NONFICTION BOOKS)

Fold a sheet of paper into fourths. In the center of the paper, write the subject of the book. Write one fact in each box. Have your child draw a picture for each fact.

BEGINNING-MIDDLE-END (FICTION BOOKS)

Fold a sheet of paper into thirds. In the first section, have your child draw and label a picture of what happened in the beginning of the story. In the second section, have your child draw and label a picture of what happened in the middle. In the third section, have your child draw and label a picture of what happened at the end of the story. Use the drawings to talk about and retell the story.

Reading together should bring curiosity and joy. Have conversations about books rather than quizzes and questioning. Remember to keep it light and fun!

QUESTIONS FOR READING COMPREHENSION

Before Reading

- What do you think this book is about?
- What do you think will happen?
- Do you think this book is real or make-believe? Why?
- What do you already know about this topic?
- What do you want to learn about this topic?

During Reading

- What do you think is going to happen next? Why?
- How do you think the book is going to end?
- Do you think this fact is interesting, funny, or strange?

After Reading

- Did you like this book? Why?
- What is your favorite part?
- Who is your favorite character?
- What is your favorite fact?

FINE-MOTOR SKILLS: MAKING HANDS STRONG

Having fine-motor skills means being able to control the small muscles of the body, including those in the fingers and hands. Fine-motor skills are needed to use a knife and fork, to screw a lid on a jar, and to use scissors. As your child develops these skills, they are better able to dress and feed themselves and to play with more intricate toys.

Fine-motor skills are especially important for learning to write. Hand strength and control is needed to hold a pencil and to form letters. You can help your child develop fine-motor skills by providing opportunities to handle and manipulate objects. Putting together puzzles, placing pegs in a board, playing board games, building with blocks, and making things from clay are all ways to build fine-motor skills. An added bonus of these activities is that they promote concentration and lengthen your child's attention span.

PENCIL GRIP

The way that children hold a pencil makes a difference. Having an efficient pencil grasp is directly related to handwriting speed and legibility. It is also less tiring for your child's hand. The goal is for your child to develop a tripod grasp. The thumb and index finger should pinch the pencil. The pencil rests on the middle finger. The back of the pencil rests on the skin between the thumb and index finger.

Try these tips for helping your child develop a tripod grip.

- Use short pencils, such as golf pencils.
- Use a thicker pencil or a triangle-shaped pencil.
- While holding the pencil, also hold a pom-pom or a coin between the ring finger and the pinky.
- Purchase a pencil gripper that helps your child position their fingers correctly.

ACTIVITIES FOR BUILDING FINE-MOTOR SKILLS

HELPING HANDS

Mealtimes are great for fine-motor practice. Children can stir, shake, chop, and mix parts of the meal. Opening and closing containers with lids also helps. Have your child set the table. Let them pour drinks into cups.

FINE-MOTOR FUN

- Use child-sized tweezers to pick up and sort pom-poms or small building blocks.
- String beads on laces or pipe cleaners.
- Have fun with chalk, paint sticks, and markers.
- Make a collage by peeling and sticking a variety of stickers on paper.
- Attach clothespins to cardboard or put them on a string for hanging pictures.
- Build shoulder strength by hanging from the monkey bars, lying on your belly when coloring, and doing wheelbarrow walks.

ROLL, SQUEEZE, AND MAKE

Handling play dough helps children build a variety of fine-motor skills. Children can form balls, roll "snakes," make a pizza and cut it with plastic scissors, and more. Try this recipe for easy homemade dough.

1. Add one cup flour, two teaspoons cream of tartar, and one-third cup table salt to a two-quart saucepan. Stir to mix.
2. Pour one cup water into a small container. Add a few drops of food coloring. Add one tablespoon vegetable oil. Stir. Add this mixture to the flour mixture in the pan.
3. Heat your burner to medium-low and stir. It will be a little lumpy, but keep stirring until the dough starts gathering around the spoon and away from the pan. This could take up to three minutes.
4. Remove mixture from saucepan and place on wax paper to cool.
5. Once cool, knead and squish the dough to remove any lumps.
6. Store in a sealed plastic bag or container.

WRITING:
HANDWRITING

Knowing how to write letters by hand smoothly, quickly, and legibly is essential for school success. Even though much schoolwork today is done on a computer, students are often asked to write by hand for jotting notes, taking tests, and completing homework. Taking time in the early grades to develop handwriting skills can prevent academic difficulties in the future.

When prekindergartners write letters at the same time they are learning letter sounds, both skills are reinforced, leading to improved reading, writing, and spelling. With practice, handwriting becomes automatic. Children don't have to think about the formation of each letter, and they are free to focus on the meaning of what they are writing.

LETTER FORMATION

Most letters can be made in one stroke. Use this guide to help your child form letters starting from the top and going to the bottom.

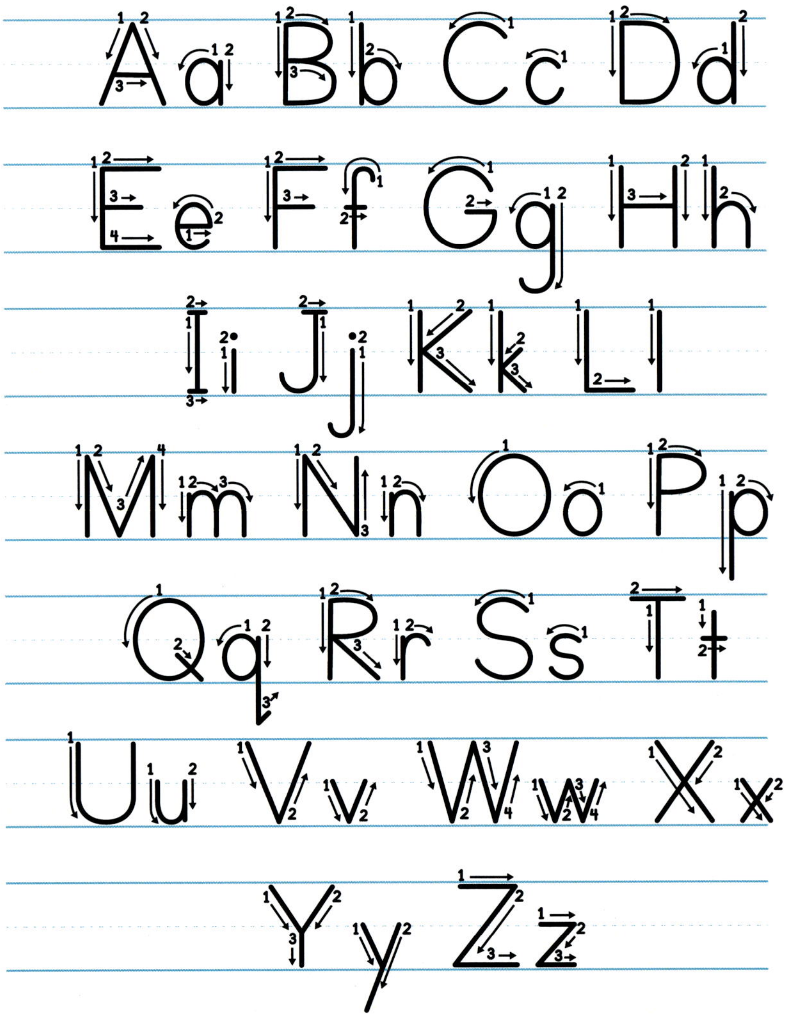

ACTIVITIES FOR BUILDING WRITING SKILLS

PREVENT CONFUSION FOR b AND d

Because lowercase *b* and *d* look so similar, children often get them mixed up. To help your child, try these tricks.

To remember the letter *b*, associate it with a bat and a ball. Write a line from top to bottom for the bat. Then, trace the line up just a little and form the circle for the ball.

To remember the letter *d*, sing the first part of the ABC song: A-B-C-D. Then, write the letter *c*, starting at the top. When you complete *c*, continue the line upward to form *d*.

TEXTURED LETTERS

Use a paintbrush dipped into liquid glue to paint a letter on a square of cardstock. Sprinkle sand or glitter on the wet glue. Allow to try, and shake off the excess material. Make additional letter cards the same way. Have your child use their finger to trace each letter and say its name and sound. Make sure to follow the correct stroke sequence shown at left.

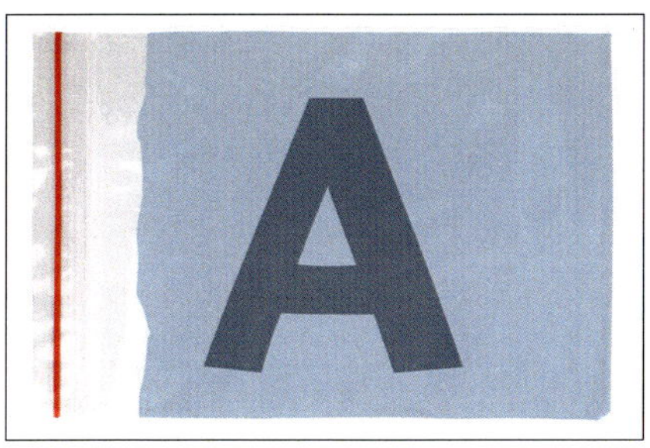

GEL WRITING

Use a black marker to write a large letter on a sheet of paper. Fill a gallon-sized resealable plastic bag with hair gel and food coloring. Flatten the bag and place it over the paper on a tabletop. Your child can use their finger to trace the letter in the gel and say its name and sound. Make sure to follow the correct stroke sequence shown at left.

WRITING: SHOWING UNDERSTANDING

When young children write, they show an awareness that printed words can tell what they want to say. Prekindergartners are making their first attempts at writing. They practice forming uppercase and lowercase letters. They use scribbling, drawing, and invented spelling to express themselves. They even learn to write the most important word of all–their name!

STAGES OF WRITING DEVELOPMENT

1. Drawing
2. Scribbling or pretend writing
3. Creating letter-like forms
4. Using invented spelling to write letters that match sounds
5. Using conventional spelling to write words

NAME-WRITING TIPS

- Teach the name of each letter in your child's name and the sound it makes.
- Start with one letter at a time and build up to the whole name.
- Show how to use uppercase letters correctly to begin a name.
- Help your child memorize the order of the letters in their first and last names.

ACTIVITIES FOR BUILDING WRITING SKILLS

SENSORY FUN

Engage your child's senses in writing practice. Have them form letter shapes by attaching small stickers or sequins to paper. Use different tools to etch letters and words into flattened play dough. Write words for your child to trace with crayons or markers in every color of the rainbow.

PICTURES ARE STORIES

Scribbling and drawing pictures are the first ways your child writes stories. Ask your child to tell you about the stories their drawings represent.

KINDERGARTEN READINESS CHECKLIST

Children who have a good start on developing pre-reading and pre-writing skills will begin kindergarten with confidence. Use this checklist as a guide of what skills to work toward. Remember that children mature at different rates. If your child cannot do everything on this list, it does not mean that they are not ready for kindergarten.

- ✔ Knows the names of uppercase (ABC) letters.
- ✔ Knows the names of lowercase (abc) letters.
- ✔ Knows the sounds of most letters.
- ✔ Can rhyme.
- ✔ Listens to a story and tells the beginning, middle, and end.
- ✔ Knows how to hold a book, turn the pages, and identify where to start reading.
- ✔ Understands that sentences are read from left to right, even if not reading yet.
- ✔ Understands simple jokes.
- ✔ Knows the names of shapes.
- ✔ Breaks a simple word into sounds (*dog* is /d/, /ŏ/, /g/).
- ✔ Says the beginning sound of a word (/b/ for *ball*).
- ✔ Says the ending sound of a word (/t/ for *hot*).
- ✔ Claps out syllables (two claps for *pancake*: pan/cake).
- ✔ Holds a crayon or pencil using a regular tripod grip.
- ✔ Draws a stick figure.
- ✔ Writes first name.
- ✔ Writes at least part of last name.
- ✔ Writes some letters of the alphabet.
- ✔ Can copy shapes +, ×, and –.
- ✔ Cuts a big circle with scissors and moves the paper while cutting the line.
- ✔ Colors a picture.
- ✔ Scribbles to write made-up words, pictures, or ideas.

Bonus Skills

- ✔ Knows the names of the days of the week.
- ✔ Knows the names of colors.
- ✔ Counts to 10 or more.
- ✔ Writes numbers 1 to 10.
- ✔ Knows age and birthdate.

WHAT TO DO WHEN YOUR CHILD STRUGGLES

As a parent, it is frustrating when your child has difficulties. When this happens, it is important to seek out help. Begin with your child's classroom teacher, who might be able to provide more personalized instruction and strategies to try at home. Tutors, professionals in private practice, and reading clinics are other ways to support your child.

If your child continues to struggle, ask the school to have a meeting that includes the classroom teacher and head of the preschool. This is an opportunity for everyone to be honest and open in a supportive way. The goal of such a meeting is to gather information in order to decide how to move forward. Some possible outcomes are formal evaluation for special education, creation of a 504 Plan or Individualized Education Plan (IEP), more intensive instruction by the classroom teacher, or referral to a pediatrician for a possible medical diagnosis.

QUESTIONS FOR TEAM DISCUSSION

- Are there attention issues at school? At home?
- Is poor attendance having an impact?
- When were the child's hearing and vision last checked?
- Does the child speak another language?
- What supports and strategies have been in place? Were they successful?
- Does the child have a medical condition that may impact learning?

WORDS TO KNOW

504 Plan: a plan that describes the accommodations that the school will provide to support the student's education

active reading: when a reader is thinking about, involved with, and engaged in a text

decoding: the ability to sound out written words

ELL: English language learner

fluency: the ability to read with speed, accuracy, and appropriate expression

high-frequency word: a word that often appears in written material and that can be decoded using common phonics rules

IEP: individualized education plan; a personalized plan that describes the special education instruction, supports, and services a child needs

literacy: the ability to read and write

phonemic awareness: the ability to identify and manipulate individual sounds in spoken words

phonics: matching the sounds of spoken English to individual letters or groups of letters; the relationship between sounds and letters

phonological awareness: the ability to identify and manipulate syllables and other parts of spoken words

reading comprehension: the ability to understand and interpret what you read

science of reading: a body of research that shows what is most important and effective in reading instruction

sight word: a word that often appears in written material and that can be difficult to decode using common phonics rules

syllable: a word part that contains one vowel sound

vocabulary: knowledge about what words mean

ADDITIONAL INFORMATION

To learn more about the science of reading:
https://teacherblog.evan-moor.com/2022/05/02/what-parents-need-to-know-about-the-science-of-reading/

To learn more about phonological awareness and phonemic awareness:
https://readingteacher.com/what-is-phonological-awareness-and-why-is-it-important/

To learn more about phonics and decoding:
https://www.twinkl.com/teaching-wiki/decoding

To learn more about vocabulary development:
https://www.edutopia.org/article/6-quick-strategies-build-vocabulary/

To learn more about reading comprehension:
https://www.readnaturally.com/research/5-components-of-reading/comprehension

To learn more about IEPs and 504 Plans:
https://www.understood.org/en/articles/the-difference-between-ieps-and-504-plans

Some information for this book came from the following websites:

- Florida Center for Reading Research https://fcrr.org
- Home Reading Helper https://www.homereadinghelper.org
- International Dyslexia Association https://dyslexiaida.org
- North Carolina Department of Public Instruction https://www.dpi.nc.gov
- Reading Rockets https://www.readingrockets.org

Written by: Madison Parker, M.Ed.
Design by: Rhea Magaro-Wallace
Series Development: James Earley
Editor: Kim Thompson

Photo credits: Shutterstock

Library of Congress PCN Data
Helping My Child with Reading Prekindergarten / Madison Parker, M.Ed.
A Guide to Supporting School Readiness Skills
ISBN 979-8-8904-2110-4 (paperback)
ISBN 979-8-8904-2120-3 (eBook)
ISBN 979-8-8904-2130-2 (ePUB)

Printed in the United States of America.

Seahorse Publishing Company
www.seahorsepub.com

Published in the United States
Seahorse Publishing
PO Box 771325
Coral Springs, FL 33077

SEAHORSE PUBLISHING